CEREMONIES OF THE DAMNED

Western Literature Series

CEREMONIES OF THE DAMNED

POEMS

ADRIAN C. LOUIS

UNIVERSITY OF NEVADA PRESS / RENO & LAS VEGAS

Western Literature Series

University of Nevada Press, Reno, Nevada 89557 USA

Manufactured in the United States of America

Book design by Carrie Nelson House

LIBRARY OF CONGRESS CATALOGING-IN-PUBLICATION DATA

Louis, Adrian C.

Ceremonies of the damned : poems / Adrian C. Louis.

p. cm. — (Western literature series)

ISBN: 978-0-87417-302-4 (paper ed. : alk. paper)

I. Title. II. Series.

PS3562.082C47 1997 97-15208

811'.54–dc21 CIP

The paper used in this book meets the requirements of American National Standard for Information Sciences—Permanence of Paper for Printed Library Materials, ANSI/NISO Z39.48-1992 (R2002). Binding materials were selected for strength and durability.

This book has been reproduced as a digital reprint.

For Colleen.

For my brothers and sisters

and for all my relations.

❖

All things considered, it's a gentle and undemanding

planet, even here. Far gentler

Here than any of a dozen other places. The trouble is

always and only with what we build on top of it.

There's nobody else to blame. You can't fix it and you

can't make it go away. It does no good appealing

To some ill-invented Thunderer

Brooding above some unimaginable crag . . .

—Lew Welch

ACKNOWLEDGMENTS

Some of these poems have been published previously, often in early versions, in *TriQuarterly, Ploughshares, New Letters, North Dakota Quarterly, The Progressive, Caliban, Cutbank, Exquisite Corpse, Red Ink, The Casper Star-Tribune, Urbanus,* and *Poetry Motel.* Other poems first saw light in *Literacy Matters: Writing in the Second Wave of Multiculturalism* (Prentice-Hall, 1997) and *Days of Obsidian—Days of Grace* (Poetry Harbor Press, 1994). "Coyote's Circle" appeared originally in *Wild Indians & Other Creatures* (University of Nevada Press, 1996). Thanks to the editors of these various publications and presses. The epigraph by Lew Welch is from "Chicago Poem," which appears in his fine collection *Ring of Bone.* Copyright ©1973 by Grey Fox Press and used with permission.

Special thanks to Trudy McMurrin, my editor at the University of Nevada Press, and a tip of the hat to Hayden Carruth, Shaun Griffin, and Bob Stewart for their help in making this project a reality. Finally, I'd like to express my gratitude to the Lila Wallace–Reader's Digest Fund for its generous support, a godsend at a troubled time.

CONTENTS

ONE : PETROGLYPHS OF SERENA

TWO : EARTH BONE CONNECTED TO THE SPIRIT BONE

THREE : THIS NEVER-ENDING FAREWELL

PETROGLYPHS OF SERENA

PART ONE

PETROGLYPHS OF SERENA

Poets behave impudently towards their experiences: they exploit them.
—Friedrich Nietzsche

In Yellowbird's Store, the tart tinge
of something sour boggles my nose.
Overpriced cans of Spaghetti-Os
and Spam on the sad shelves
are powdered with Great Plains dust.
In Yellowbird's Store, winter people
are hooked up to video poker
machines for brief transfusions.
The faint whispers of dreams and desires
fade with each coin thrown away.
Some Indians prefer gambling to making love.
Not me. I love to graze on the sparse, black
cornsilk in the valleys of the Sioux
and it will be my downfall.

Six-twenty in the morning. These Dakota stars
are as blanched as dead minnows floating
on a garish pink and blue sea of daybreak.
I shake my head, light a Marlboro,
and scope my wife getting dressed.
She can't cook worth a damn,
is incredibly and increasingly forgetful.
But she loves me and treats me as good
as a recovering drunk deserves.
Nevertheless, I'm thinking of the wondrous
and drool-making beauty of my student Serena
who is flunking but would get an A-plus
and my fuzzy soul if she asked.

Unlike parched Christ on his cross,
my mouth was watering.
Sitting on the front porch, I saw the snot
yellow moon dishevel two Kleenex clouds.
A clichéd stray dog down by the creek

was alternating keys of hunger and horror.
It would soon be suppertime.
I fired up a smoke and sucked it greedily.
The dancing coal lost itself
in the star blanket of night.
In the house my tired wife
was frying venison steaks.
My mouth was watering,
but I wasn't hungry at all.
I was dreaming of Serena.
Dark Serena with her broken English.
Wild-ass Serena and our Indian dance
of self-destruction.

Friday is a blistering prairie day.
105-degree heat will dissolve the will
of the people and tonight you'll see all hues
of brown swarming over this dusty soil.
Many of these people will be scarred.
Some of them will be magna cum laude
graduates of the S.D. State Pen.
Some will be young and lost for the first
time and some will be old and dying.
All will be thirsty. Parched and tough.
Tonight there is bound to be trouble.
I can hardly wait. Lord,
how lust becomes me.
I will be there and so will Serena.

The old people said bad spirits blew in
with the west wind and would not leave
no matter how much they prayed.
The old people said the air was bad.
Death danced through the front doors
of many houses that winter, and finally
spring sent children wild upon the earth.
Death ran from the sharp glee in their eyes.

Death ran from the sex breath of summer.
Finally, Serena was with me.
We were naked, biting each other hard
and the air, oh, the air was good
and I drank it in without
the slightest cough of guilt.

And then it was winter again.
Oh, man, a desperate Dakota winter.
Our neighbors shot a starving deer
behind their HUD house
and butchered it in their front yard.
They wrapped large pieces in Hefty bags
and stored them in the trunk
of their broken-down '72 Olds.
In February they ran out of wood so they
burned chunks of old tires in the woodstove.
Their children went to school smudged
and smelling like burnt rubber.
A typical hard-ass Dakota winter.
All across the Rez, wild Indians
shiver-danced around woodstoves
and howled the most wondrous songs
of brilliant poverty.

Lust comes with a darkblood price.
This is how darkness comes to me.
Serena's late for speech class as usual.
Everyone's done their demos but her:
Ain't got none. I'm sorry, but
I just come from working
on a friend's brokedown car.
Then said (in a sly-shy-sneaky kind of way)
she could demo how to clean a carburetor.
Outside in the bed of her pickup.
Well . . . Okay. (What the hell could I say?)
so the whole class trudges

out upon the jagged-ice earth.
It's dark, crazy, she has no flashlight, so
I let her use my new white plastic one.
She GUMS-OUT the carb. Slaps in a new kit.
We're all freezing ass. This is Indian education?
Above, the nosey, twinkling stars are giggling.
I give her a C for effort. Would've been higher,
but she decorated my new flashlight
with big, fat greaseprints. I tell you now that
the next week I hear she's drunk-rolled
a car and is dead, just like that—dead,
so I buy a new flashlight.
A red one.
I take a drive through the deserted Badlands
late at night and stop.
I turn on the old flashlight she used
and toss it in some sage beside the road.
It glows in my rearview mirror
for miles before it finally vanishes.

The old people were moving slowly
through the cold air like exhausted swimmers
fighting the tides of a lung-raping sea.
But, the sun had its high beams on
and near the creek children were laughing
and moving as fast as spit on a hot woodstove.
Grandfather, it was a good day to pray.
Grandfather, it was a good day to pray
that the young would somehow get to be old.
Above all, it was a good day to die.
I did not know her family that well so
I watched her burial from a distance.
Old Indian . . . trick.
Middle-aged Indian . . . trick.

About a year after Serena
died in the car wreck

I saw her again—sort of spooky, but
ghost sightings are common around here.
Spirits come and go, to and fro.
She was with some strange-looking Skins,
drove a different car, and looked puzzled,
half-angry when I waved at her.
Acted like she didn't know me.
Kind of gave me a kiss-my-butt look
and then flipped me the bird.
I shrugged and did the same back to her.
Her car was filled with buffalo heads,
stampeding the ghost road
to White Clay.

Driving the sheet-ice reservation roads,
ground blizzards whirl and blind. Underneath
all, something paleolithic begs fidelity.
It is something deep inside the hardened fist
of almost every Indian man I know.
It is not an unquenchable thirst to live
free from red tape and plastic.
Brothers, you know it is not trickster
dreams or buffalo visions.
It isn't self-determination or the good red road.
It is the unending whisper of the ancestors.
It is that simple urge to scalp a white man.
I think it has something to do with love.
The sweet, sweet squeak
of blade hitting headbone.
The snapdance of sinew
yanked awry.

Near here, over by those dead cottonwoods, is
where I picked up the lady hitchhiker last winter.
Oh, she laughed and talked Skin sexy
after I gave her a cigarette and a beer.
Near Wolf Creek turnoff I glanced

over to where she was sitting.
She'd vanished. The seat was empty.
My heart beat brilliant.
I began to sweat and then shook
like lemon Jell-O.
Up the road, I saw a deer dash past.
Its eyes were smiling, and a cigarette
dangled from its red-painted lips.
Its eyes were Serena's.

Newly minted leaves sparkle
on the giant cottonwoods.
It's the first pow-wow of the season.
They say even a white man can listen closely
and understand how the drum is our heart.
It pounds and pulses these words through
the blood of our Indian Nations:
"We have survived. Yes, we have survived.
Look at us dancing. Look at us laughing.
God damn you *wasicus,* we'll always survive!"
Yes, they say *even* a white man can listen closely
and understand how the drum is our heart.

The sign here on this bar used to say
NO INDIANS ALLOWED but that wasn't true.
Hey, we know that was not true at all.
Here, the white traders made a fortune
taking savage souls in payment
for pints of whiskey and wine.
Here, countless stumbling Skins entered
the gates of the Fire Water World.
If you listen closely, you can hear their ghosts
winging and whimpering through
the dark skies of this dying America.
Brothers, I swear to Christ on his cross
if you open your mouth, you can taste
their rain of ghost tears.

❖

We are all hiding from the truth.
Our children have no respect
because their parents cannot connect
the values of the ancient chiefs
to the deadly grief that welfare brings.
We're reaping the womb's reward of mutant
generations who stumbled toward dismembering
the long and sometimes senile span between you,
Great Spirit, and your artwork, man.
The question is, can the children be saved?
And if so, then why? Will they ever be whole
or do we just add them to the dark days
of casualties from Sand Creek
to Ira Hayes?

I mean, do we catalogue them
in the first grade and then sit back
and wait, afraid that one will be dead
in a car wreck at ten? That one has a room
reserved at the state pen?
That one will flunk out of college
a total of eight times over a ten-year slate
and then will take his life after stabbing
his kids, his dad, his wife?
That one will have six children,
none from the same man,
and all will carry their mom's surname?
That one will move to a city and drink
so much that his heart will forget
the prayer of human touch?
That one will write their story
and end it as if it were
a lousy job he just quit
without searching
for a space to inject
the slightest hint of grace?

❖

What we never say is that when we hit
rock-bottom, we can still drop farther.
She said back in the old days
we took care of our elders.
There was no AFDC, no food stamps.
We had gardens, we hunted.
We respected our parents
and we weren't afraid of work.
In the old days, men did not beat
their women for no reason.
In the old days, children had two parents.
Yes, in the old days life was better.
In the old days I was young and in love,
she said with a shrug . . . so I kissed her.
On Serena's mother's old,
cracked fullblood lips
I kissed her ever so softly.

Inside this shack the restless spirit
of a woman will put on a faded shawl
and take a kerosene lamp
from atop a battered bureau.
She will open the door and float
through the chilled air to the outhouse.
She will spread the light into all the corners
making sure no spiders lurk.
Then she will sing to herself and dream
of running water and porcelain.
That is what this spirit will do. I know.
She is the grandmother
of us all.

Wanbli Gleska Wi (Thalia) said
old-time Lakota call it *wasigla.*
A woman must mourn for a full year
to pay respect to the spirit of the departed.

Not supposed to leave the house,
have to wear black,
can't go shopping or go pow-wow.
Just stay home and mourn.
When a woman is spirit-keeping or
ghost-keeping, she can't make sudden
moves—especially with her hands.
Can't disturb the air.
And has to put out food
at each meal to feed the spirit.
One full year, Serena's younger sister
Thalia said in my motel room.
Must never offend the spirits, Thalia said.
Must *never* offend the spirits, Thalia said,
or bad shit will happen to you.
Traditional Indian wisdom, she said.
What goes around comes around
or should it be
what comes around goes around?
You don't believe that, do you? I asked.
Nothing bad would happen to me.
I laughed and got undressed,
safe and guilt-free
in the snug, smug darkness
of lust.

EARTH BONE CONNECTED TO THE SPIRIT BONE

PART TWO

EARTH BONE CONNECTED TO THE SPIRIT BONE

Where is the Life we lost in living? —T. S. Eliot

When America died, I was passed out
and never noticed. Was it a meteor
or an invisible wand that waved past
our eyes and blinded everyone?
Thalia had left for Los Angeles two years
before and I was still married, Indian-style.
I awoke one morning and electrical maggots
were spurting from the mind-control machine
in our disheveled living room.
We were off the Rez in Rushville, Nebraska,
eighteen miles south of Pine Ridge.

Under the carcinogenic mist of cropdusters,
this lame-brained bordertown staggers and
smiles so senselessly.
What remains of America here
is quickly dying. There is only one lonely
restaurant—at the bowling alley—serving
skanky, subhuman food to seed-capped patrons.
The high school team is nicknamed
"The Longhorns." The steaks and hamburger
in the largest grocery store in town
are often greener than the Third World, yet
stockyards are a stone's throw from Main St.
This is the heart of cattle country.
A ripened, diseased American heart.
The days seem darker in this small white town.
From eighteen miles south, I watch
the Rez gangbangers come to town—pallid, goofy
reflections of the gang scum they've seen on TV.
Sedated by sweating daylight, they rise
to moonlight's murderous soul.
Broken, the sacred circle is.

Broken, the sacred circle is
light years from mending.
We all play Indian roulette.
Red fluid of life. Black fluid of death.
My wheel spins into middle-aged sameness.
Still, there's something I want to say about love.
It *is* the cruellest drug, and I've used and abused it
and now I'm spinning, afraid to die alone or
together. And we're all the same, even our
leaders, the tribal politicians. These chiefs are big
brown ants in panties. Flint-skinned mutants
of the sacred song. Insects.
Hear me. Where is our HUD house?
Where are our warriors?
Where are the ancestor spirits
who should be guiding us?
Where is the love?

O Reservation. Home, home, hell. Eighteen
miles north resides our howl and hovel
where everything changes except the rusty
bars across the moon.
Listen, listen to the rabid coyote in the frozen
Badlands. It's singing a lovesong to us.
An itchy cowboy and Indian tune.
We can hear it at this Nebraska Street Dance.
Yeeeeeee-hawwwwww! Sad, broken cowpokes
are bootscooting over the hot pavement.
Huge, hairy galoots, veritable Blutos under straw
Stetsons. On horses by day,
on heifers tonight.

And glimmering in the eastern mist
is that Oz called Lincoln, Nebraska.
Beyond green cornfields that white city gleams.
Midwestern Cambridge. Home of *Cliffs Notes.*
City of lame, homespun poets and other plains
jokers. The catapult where state income taxes

launch Husker thugs to Orange Bowls. Great
American city with a parched cornfield soul:
O rasping generic America. Home of the hospital
we visit and leave with pills to flower false hope.

My wife is upstairs on Cognex, Prozac, and Haldol.
I'm forty-eight years old and groggy
from napping after self-flagellation.
The two Bible thumpers at the front door
graze on my plump nakedness. God help me
if you can, I mumble at them.
I'm scaling the black glass canyons of hell
and doing tolerably well, almost enjoying myself
as they titter and quickly turn
whiter than white.
Later I wish I'd thought to ask them
why is their God punishing me?

Satan blessed our Indian democracy.
The red sun rises.
Since the diagnosis, neither of us works.
The bathtub is yellow. The bills are white.
They mount and mount, as does my collection
of books—writers I don't know send me their books
from every corner of this mad nation.

I used to let you read their words, but now you
read the same lines over and over, and
I'm too bitchy caring for you to read aloud.
Our fieldstone basement is crumbling
under the weight of their books.
I wish they'd send money, not books.

You have taken to wandering.
Vanished for the third time this month.
You're out there someplace shimmering

in your own haze of dead memory.
It does no good to call the cops.
I've learned my lesson.
Twice they've called me to retrieve you
from the grocery store where you
circled aisles, your cart loaded down
with catfood and canned soup.
So, I sit and wait for your return,
trying the mindless anesthetic of MTV.
I watch the music in black and white.
In Seattle young grunge nihilists
are experiencing impotence before their time.
In L.A. ebonical rappers sing grunts of the
vengeful cock—a sad, self-demonizing
urban drugthug lingo that reservation
kids are now mouthing, too.
Rap scares me. How is it possible to age with
grace? Where is the desperado I was?
Where are you now, my love?
And how is it still possible for me to hate?
Worn by the daily agitation of your slow-motion
terminal disease, I retain my anger.
I turn off the tube and think of one enemy in
particular. The bastard is thirteen years older
than me and I will not be speaking ill
of the dead when I piss on his grave.
I will be merely dousing the white devils
which possessed him. Their names
were greed, lust, and booze. He was the me
before I met you.

Still waiting, I call my friend Verdell
to see if he's seen her.
He asks to borrow money.
He needs medicine to get well
but no, no money, Cousin.
You already owe me.
No, I ain't giving you no twelve-step quick-step.

Only the bottom, hard, harsh, and swift.
Then you get up or don't, either one better than
now. Oh, how you love living death.
Oh, how you live loving death.
Verdell said he fell down and broke his crown
and awoke at the V.A. hospital in a room filled
with decrepit old men in wheelchairs.
"I was one of them," he said and chuckled.

So I said to Verdell:
"The information superhighway leads
to consciousness overflowing the toilet
or true denial.
The murderous nature of man
craves Nature's death.
I know where you're coming from, Verdell.
Every day I also fight the urge to drink,
especially now that my wife's so sick.
Every minute of every day.
Sometimes I think: what if I got cancer?
If I did, the first one to know would be a
bartender—I'd be just like you, again."

Then after an insufferable silence, Verdell said
at least he wasn't coughing up blood,
but he did go into seizures:
"The earth was dying—and its children, too.
The earth was dying—and its children, too."

I'm sweating bullets at the Social Security
office in the nearest small city.
This homely white woman's got me bent
over her desk and is banging me good.
No, we're not legally married, I tell her.
No, I'm not her legal guardian.
(Just approve the damn papers, please.)
Christ!—I just wish someone would've asked
this bureaucrat to her high school prom.

Government mutants like her
are all the same. Their souls are powdered milk
and poor people are the water they crave.
In the curdled muddle of my own midlife, I
whitewash all her fatalistic interrogatives.
I tell her that here is no primeval carnage
of carcasses in caves. I was born poor
and will die the same. The primal
no longer exists—the black crust entombing
blood lies upon a sesame seed bun.
Yes, I tell her, I am part of plastic America,
but I'm no holy man among the hollow men.
In my time I've worshipped at the altar of greed.
If I possessed the true
Holy Grail, I'd only drink beer from it.
Oh, sad, gray fed employee, please free
us both from these minutes of madness.

I come and go like the pavement in winter.
No longer greaseblack at the intersection
of blood leaves and salt-peppered snow,
I sometimes dye my sideburns, my soul.
Ancestors appear and disappear.
What the white people don't know
is that the Ghost Dance really worked.
My dogs are turning gray and swimming
slowly throughout the house.
There were many women I loved, but I
think they all had the same name.
I love you. I love you. They were all you
and now you are slowly vanishing.

Vanishing . . .
From a bleached fencepost aimed at the
gunpowder sky, an eagle explodes upward.
Our car is speeding down the black-ice road
when we see a small plume dancing earthward.
Your circle is almost full.

That is the message of the feather, yet I continue
to pretend that I don't understand it.
Our dreadful curse of middle age
is no joking matter, but I smile
and hide in cliché: We're no longer young
and my mind can't grasp that fact.
In your mind there is not one truth,
but many truths. There are no lies—just
Nutty-Putty warpings of the truth.
Once I told you I learned all the English
I needed in eight-ball and snooker
and you understood.

Now you cannot begin to comprehend
that you are dying *and* that you are not dying.
I wish I could have you do the rest.
This is your poem. The failed words are mine.
All your worlds are fading, and I'm flailing
because it's getting so hard to love you.
Do you understand? I'm not sure I do.
I remember your father said, "Long as I
can remember, us Indians leased
our land to the white man."
He said, "The *wasicu* grows hay and gets rich."
He used to run circles around these hay bales
when he was a kid getting in shape for high
school basketball—the famed 1936 State Champs.
He said, "Sometimes, just at dusk, these hay bales
look like ghosts of the buffalos or . . . something,
you know?"

Darling, it seems my only reason
for living is to help you remember.
All I can do is set up situations
and then point the finger a pouty,
porkhearted fairy recently wrote.
Sweetheart, do you recall that tourist
who said how come at every pow-wow

you honor the American flag?
This has always been a puzzle to me, he said.
You are the people who fell through
the crack in the Liberty Bell.
You're always the first to invoke
the Washita River or Bosque Redondo
or Wounded Knee when you
perceive injustice against your people.
God, despite this, you still love to honor the flag.
I just don't get it, the tourist said to us.
There was no way to answer him. What could
we say? Someone said Sitting Bull said:
If the Great Spirit had desired me to be
a white man, he would have made me so
in the first place. It is not necessary
for eagles to be crows.

Most of us know Sitting Bull wasn't bullshitting,
but we still don't know which way to go.
We are torn between two different worlds and
between the past and the future. At least that's
what we tell ourselves when we fail. We
never mention the fact that it was Skins
who killed Mr. Bull.

On Sundays the caterwauling from
the holy-roller church down the street
is fearless, fearful, and fearsome.
In that eternal fear
they call Christian love, they yodel to forget
who they are and screech the wondrous lie
that all of us are their God's children.
If their God is real, why won't he help us?
We pay taxes here, too. It's all a bland joke.
I've heard these same poor whites say Skins
don't want to work and curse us, sputtering
if it weren't for welfare and government
handouts, we'd starve to death.

And on Friday nights I've seen flocks
of these angel-addled sodbusters drunk
and desperately scheming for Indian pussy.
Yes, I can set up situations and point my finger.
Last winter a mid-February thaw startled cows
into dropping early calves onto the muddy
plains—even trees were tricked into budding.
That week a cop in Gordon, Nebraska, murdered
an Indian guy. Shot him square in the back and
got away with it. When I was young I could
always tell who the real cowboys were.
They always smelled like cowshit.
These days they wear nylon panties,
are computer literate, and draw their guns
as if their redneck lives had honor.
God damn this chapped-ass cowboy hell.

Once the Rez sun rose bloated and angered.
Like a neglected child, it pouted over
the purple hills around Pine Ridge Village.
Dogs ran looking for cars to crush them.
Soon it would be too hot to do anything but find
shade and suffer, yet Adrian would survive.
He had enough beer stocked up to get drunk
and sleep through the heat of the day
and get drunk again at night.
Adrian was one smart Indian alkie.
A flesh and blood oxymoron.
O sweetheart, remember?
Please remember.

Your brothers have you for the weekend.
My ancient mower refuses
to eat any more lawn.
It belches and shudders and quits.
The rusty steel teeth have had their fill.
Sweating dusk sedates me

so I nap on the couch
and wake to the pine-goosed moon.
With aching old muscles and a young heart
slightly crazed by my own funk and thirst,
I head out for the Stockman's Saloon.
It's quiet there when I walk in
and order a nonalcohol beer
and a *Rapid City Journal.*
In this newspaper made from flesh of trees
I read about the ongoing O.J. circus in LA.
In another life I lived and loved in that mutant
world, in that yellow air and maddening din.
The bartender peers at my paper and mutters
that L.A. deserves a thermonuclear enema. He's
white and has green teeth. Me, I'd cast my vote
for Las Vegas or maybe murderous Serbia.
But then what do I know?
I can only set up situations and point my finger.

Like the pale professor who claimed
to be Cherokee. She was in over her head,
spelunking in baleen when she decried
the whiteness of the whale and scrimshawed
the blackboard. My sad soul tittered at her
blubber butt jiggling.
The poor woman would never see that
Melville's big fish was an Indian whale.
I should've let her taste the ripe redness
of my hapless harpoon. Yippie-ki-yi-yo.
I should've bowed, kissed her hand
and whispered that before he shipped out with
Ahab, Queequeg had his lonely sperm frozen.
And that I am one of his clones.

Everywhere I look there are sad fools
pretending they understand Indians.
Indians don't even understand Indians.

I've said it all before
and I have written *this* several times before,
but again I say that downtown, inside
the Rez post office, a poster displays new stamps:
romantic Indian war bonnets in hues
never seen by our ancestors.
Outside, bruised and bumbling winos trek
by with Hefty bags full of flattened cans.
Again I say that when Crazy Horse was murdered
at Fort Robinson, the last living free Indian died.
Except for me, darling. Except for me, sweetheart.
All my life I have been young, and this year I no
longer am. The summer is putrid, and I'm toying
with seven years of dry behavior.
Sweating and drinking near beer,
I'm in the oven of a bordertown bar
and I don't know why I crawled in
except to not think of you and yet
you're the only thing on my mind.
The air is harsh and purple.
I'm wedged in a narrow passage.
It's sad-black and scurrying sounds
are dancing in the darkness.
I know Jehovah's in a coma so I'm praying
to the television, yes, God damn it,
I'm praying to Phil Donahue
that I won't start drinking:
Help me, Phil. Let me free to be me! I'm
an Indian morsel trapped in the guts
of a cannibal called America who,
for rabid religious reasons and a touch
of trickle-down economics, has shoved
a pickle past its tight sphincters.
I don't want to drink. I don't want to point
my finger anymore. I only want silence,
but in this church the deadening Mass
of my wife's brain oblivion
is pounding louder than hell.

❖

Earth bone connected to the spirit bone.
That's what I say in the chest-pain night.
Heart bone connected to the ghost bone.
And I pray that I could take all man's
infirmities of flesh, all the little cancers,
the tooth cavities, the blackheads,
the failing kidneys, the wrinkling skin,
the allergies, the clogged arteries, the aphasias,
take all those bad things from one's body, suck
them out by cosmic means, compress all those
negatives into a compact ball of black star mass
and hurl it into the sun.
Then I would pray that the molten-golden
dew of love would cover this land.

But life is not TV.
We cannot remove decay.
Still, it is the wish of newness we desire.
The sunken couch arises, the flickering TV
becomes clear, the dog-stained rug fresh,
and the scratched walls painted . . . but life
is not so TV-easy. And no.
No molten-golden dew of love
will ever cover this land.
Ponce de León was not searching for gold
when he came trudging up the Everglades
humming papal torture songs. We know
he was searching for a "fountain of youth."
And so what (in my hours of darkness,
when the computer of memory scrolls
sad ancient flashbacks)
do I focus on, wish a return to?
A moment of stolen sex, or an accidental
hand-touching, or the wistful glance of some
unrequited love? Maybe a touchdown pass
in a high school football game? No!
For the most part, I seem to want to return

to pained points of failure. Earth bone
connected to the spirit bone . . . and often
the doors of memory are of no consequence.

I, Adrian, live in the land of the common
doorbell. Every time the doorbell rings
on a TV commercial, my dogs go wild and I
jump up off the couch looking for a place to hide.
Me, a middle-aged man acting like it's 1962.
1962 and I'm a sophomore in high school.
It's Saturday and I'm in my cubby hole of a room
off the enclosed porch of the old railroad house
whacking off when the dogs start barking.
I see a pickup churning up our dirt road.
I'm in my sanctuary, connecting my groin
bone to the heaven bone.
I do not worry until there is a pounding
on the small pine door to my room.
My Nutty-Putty heart ricochets around
my halfbreed ribcage. I pull up my pegged Levi's
and peek out the door. There is Chris Brandon,
fellow soph. A white boy, dressed in his usual
crisply starched button-down clothes.
I smell the Vitalis on his flat-top with wings.
He's no friend, just someone I pass in the halls,
but what the hell is he doing here?
On the porch outside my room is a bucket
of soiled diapers from one of my little sisters.
The entire corridor is swamped with shit-smell.
The whole house is in dirty disarray.
Burning shame makes my eyeballs flutter.
In the living room I can see my illiterate,
drunken, white stepfather making small talk
with Brandon's father. My brown mother
is scurrying after the smaller kids
and she's wearing a tattered gingham dress.
Her black hair is electric and she's pregnant,
although the baby she's holding is less

than a year old and the flypaper above
my head is so covered with flies
that it couldn't hold another and worst of all,
I've still got a boner, and Brandon looks
down and spots it.
At that instant I pray for nuclear attack.
A complete devastation of mankind,
of Adrian, of Brandon, of my entire known
world existing in the midst
of that Nevada Indian poverty
thirty-three years ago.

So, I live in the land of the common doorbell.
I live in the land of the common death.
This *is* still Indian country and it is to
the Indian spirits that I must pray.
I must fill our home with prayer.
Death and madness are hovering
above our house.
I have a desperate and honest need of prayer.
Earth bone connected to spirit bone.
I must pray for the woman I love.
Her very mind is vanishing.
I must burn sweet grass, sage,
and pray with the pipe.
And so now I pray:

Grandfather of the West—
Who lives in the setting sun of my birth,
in the red blood air of my birth
I'm praying to you.
Pity me. Help me, please.
Help me to help another whose mind
is evaporating like rain on these July plains.
Help me to help another who truly needs
my help. With this first clump of tobacco
into the pipe, I pray for her.

Grandfather of the North—
Grandfather of this land
of the pines and bitter winds.
Take pity on me. I do not pray for myself.
I'm praying for wholeness
for all of us thus fractured.
We are many, Grandfather.
We are ghost warriors in the setting sun,
an endless army of broken Skins.
This second clump of tobacco goes in the pipe.

Grandfather of the East—
Who lives where the sun rises
and darkness is eased.
This third clump is for you.
Again, I pray for wholeness and for sanity.
I pray for all of us who need your help.
I pray for a woman who needs your healing.
She is a good woman, your Indian daughter.
She's made her mistakes, but her heart is good.
Upon all that is holy, I say she is kind.
Upon all that is holy, she deserves to be
whole.

Grandfather of the South—
One toward whom we all face.
I pray for recovery, for a healing
for someone I love dearly but who is
quickly becoming someone I do not know.
This is not a prayer for myself. Please listen,
Grandfather. This fourth clump of tobacco
is for you. Help her please.

Grandfather, who is the Great Spirit—
One whom I call *Numanah,* and my woman
calls *Tunkasila,* I pray to you.
You are the Creator, you are the Great Spirit.
You are our God. Pity me. Help me.

Help me to be a good, strong man
to an ailing woman.
This fifth clump is to open your ears.

Grandmother Earth—
Mother of us all. I pray to you, I pray for your
feminine assistance. Pity me. Help me.
Help me to help one of your daughter-sisters.
And now the pipe is loaded. Now it is ready to
be smoked. And now a second round of prayers.
It is needed. Dear spirits, it is needed.

Oh Spirits of the West Wind—
Receive this pipe and have pity on your people.
From you comes the Thunderbird who purifies
the *inipi* and the earth. You correct our mistakes.
We are frail and weak humans and
we sometimes do not do things right.
You keep us from doing wrong. You are the
giver of rain and the beginning of life.
The thunder of your Horse People
from the Black Mountains fills us with awe.
You are mighty. Send the Black Eagle to help us.
We await your arrival.

Spirits of the North—
You live in the sacred Red Mountains.
From you comes the good red road
—the holy road of our people.
It is with you the Sacred Buffalo Calf Woman
stands. It is you who lead the Buffalo People
out of lost darkness. Help me be strong and
steady under this adversity. Enable me to walk
the good red road with a straight face.
Let me not talk out of both sides of my mouth.
Let me truly be humble and honest. Show me
the starlight path that leads to the good land.
Send your messenger the Golden Eagle

to guide me. Help me as I pray to you
with your sacred pipe.
I'm praying for one I love who,
in her frailty, needs my love and strength.

Spirits of the East—
From you comes the Morning Star
which radiates wisdom.
From you comes the sun filling
our dark world with light.
From you comes the moon that gives
us help and protection at night.
I have been unfaithful and dishonest,
yet I know that in your Yellow Mountains
powerful Elk People shake their great horns.
Send the Bald Eagle and help me gain
wisdom that I may find the things
to do and say to help
the sad lady I love. This is my need.
This is what I pray for.

Spirits of the South—
Land where all living things face, where all
the animal spirits live, forgive me
and turn your face toward me.
Send your messenger, the White Crane.
Help me, in my need, help me to help
the one I love. Help me to be strong
for her and not against her.
And don't let my fear turn to anger.

Grandfather, Great Spirit—
Accept this humility as my true state
and not some conjured prayer stick.
You are powerful and above all things.
All things come from you.
You are the most holy.
You *are* the most holy.

Let your Spotted Eagle
look down upon me
and hear my prayer.
I do believe you can do all things.

Grandmother Earth—
It is from you that we come,
and it is to your arms
that one day we shall return.
From you comes all that grows.
You give us the medicine plants,
the winged creatures, the four-legged,
the things that swim and crawl.
Grandmother, help me, for I am pitiful.
It is to your brown, warm arms that one day
we shall return, Grandmother,
but for the one I love this is not the time.

Spirits,
I smoke this pipe and pray to you.
My earth bone is connected
to your spirit bone.
I pray for all my people,
for all my relations,
but for one in particular.

And so it begins or ends . . .
My hopeful heart is a red balloon
floating up toward the red spirits.
My heart bone is my prayer bone.
These words are more than blood or tears.
My earth bone *is* connected to the spirit bone.
The rest is up to the spirits because
all life is controlled by the spirits.

I listen to the ghost talk of tumbleweeds,
nightcrawling, rasping across the dry
desert heart of my distant homelands.
I listen and listen, but there is no real amen.

Then a word comes, an English word
with harsh Germanic overtones.
It is a large word that rises
from this dusty prairie soil
and reaches high into the blazing sunset.
This solitary word comes and erases
the connection between my earth bone
and spirit bone.
This word is Teutonic and Nazi-sounding.
This word is Alzheimer's.
And now, fuck all the words
we've ever uttered,
it becomes the only word
in our world.

THIS NEVER-ENDING FAREWELL

PART THREE

ALZHEIMER'S

I'm in the waiting room
and you're in the magnetic resonance imager.
I guess they're photographing your soul
(or what remains of it)
but it doesn't take an MRI to discern
the red pentimento beneath
the fast-food landscape of Rapid City.

I slink out to sneak a smoke.
The lushness of ripe corn, Big Macs
and cowcrap blended onto the palette
of winter dusk and then brushed
over the red-necked symmetry
of these squat buildings cannot hide
the fact that this is Indian ground.
A night sky full of redmen died
so this arrogant city could thrive.
This small pimple on the white butt
of America is haunted, truly haunted
by the red ghosts of sunset, darling,
but waxing political is pointless.
And memory now seems nothing more
than the cruel glue that binds
mankind to God.
You're having your brain scanned
so we can know for sure
if you're spinning a cocoon
for your new empty mind.

THIS ENDS WITH A FROZEN PENIS

for Martín Espada

Once we could talk like long-lost friends.
The very warp of words
and ideas welded us together.
Now, very little of what I say registers,
though you say you understand
when I point the finger of blame
and spin into minor pyrotechnics.
Anymore, most all I do is rework the alphabet
into black banners of retribution.
We are on the couch watching Loni Anderson
promote her kiss-and-tell book about her
pained life with Burt Reynolds.
When you say you never liked Burt, I tell you
that I truly am a holy man of lesser vengeance.
They are showing film clips of Burt.
Look at him now on the tube, I say.
The old fool is chaotic, decrepit, destitute.
His goofy-looking wig is askew
and he's acting like the ghost
worms of youth are biting and breeding
beneath his liverspotted skin.
Yes, I did this to him. Honest to God.
Okay, I did use the sacred pipe.
I invoked the Thunder Beings
from the west wind.
I brought forth Skinwalkers
and all the slinking wrath
of the shadows we fear.
I used black tobacco ties.
My altar held the deadly claws of owl.
My smudging fan was made
from the tail of raven.
I shot the arrows of bad medicine.
I shot the arrows of black medicine
into Burt Reynolds' bad actor's heart.
And why? You understand, but

those hairless little hermaphrodites
of the cognitive elite probably don't.
Well, I did it because he claimed to be part
Indian and I never bought that for a minute.
I did it because my education
would never allow me to digest
his good-old-boy celluloid cretinism.
I did it because your memory is fading.

Listen, how Indians really are is . . .
is if we get educated, I mean leave
the reservation and go to a good school,
get a couple of degrees, then come back,
we see how hopeless things really are.
So then we go away to another place
to teach white students about us Indians
and we focus on the positive, the good
old-time culture, and we know
we will never go home,
that home has been educated out of us.
When they cut our hair at the boarding schools
and dressed us in machine-made clothes,
the map to home was lost.
Just ask Jim Thorpe.

But, I digress . . .
I really did it because I loved Loni.
This was long before I met you.
In Cincinnati, on WKRP, she was
my heartland Helen of Troy.
Oh, how I used to dream that one day
she would snake her arm out of the tube
and have her way with me.
Yes, I also did it because I suspected
Burt drained her life force.
Burt was the first American
vampire I ever recognized.
Maybe I did it because with each passing
year I retreat deeper into
the concentric circles of meaning.

With each year, I find
myself farther from truth.
I castigate him, but I am a phony too.
I can't even do what I'd truly like—
to enter bookstores and forge signatures
in the books of writers I loathe
and then add vile, shocking tidbits
like: *Castrate every American*
who pilots a snowmobile!

Yes, I'm as shallow as Burt.
I don't know why some people think
I own some clues to the mystery of life.
Yesterday, listening to country
and western KSDZ in Gordon, Nebraska,
I heard the twangy D.J. say his fantasy
was to be locked in the back of a beer truck
for twenty-four hours with Loni.
Now what was that redneck moron thinking?
Wouldn't it be too pud-puckering
cold back there? And even if Loni consented
to doing the deed (which she wouldn't
—YOU KNOW SHE WOULD NOT!)
what would they use for a bed?
Who would want to make love
atop chilled cases of brew?
And would they both guzzle
suds all that time? Jesus, darling,
remember how we used to swill?
And how would this bumpkin react
if Loni had to tinkle?

Probably none of this really matters.
Besides, locked in the back of a beer truck,
that D.J. would find out it's pitchblack.
He wouldn't even be able to see Loni.
Thus, why Loni at all?
Surely her good looks made her his choice.
In the dark, Loni might as well be Janet Reno,

our manly, florid-faced attorney general.
Lord, imagine banging the "Butcher of Waco"
in the back of a beer truck!

But please, darling, I'm not saying
it's all the same in the dark.
Just that on earth a billion
or so married men spurt spunk
to the dream dolls of their dim minds.
I suppose this is one of the ways we pray,
and O God, I did it because . . . Well,
I never liked his designer jeans
and cowboy boots and I never did believe
he was a good football player.
He was too much of a pretty boy.
Hard to imagine Burt doing the forearm
shiver or wind sprints and tackling dummies.
And just what THE HOLY HELL was he doing
diddling Dinah Shore just when she should've
been sliding gracefully into old age?
To wit, I did it because I didn't like his laugh,
his wig, his swagger, his aimless cocksure banter.
That is why I used black medicine.
O see him now! See Burt, poor Burt—
chaotic, destitute, decrepit. And me?
Pretty much like him, but mission accomplished.
My mad middle-aged mission is accomplished
so I switch the channel, appeased.
We watch the Mormon Tabernacle Choir
singing Christmas carols
and I sigh as you sing along.
The camera pans the Temple in Salt Lake.
The snow-covered Wasatch Mountains
bulge in the background.
Wasatch is the Ute Indian word for "frozen penis."
You smile cuckoo and giggle.
You smile cuckoo
and tell me to hush.
And I take your hand and do as you ask.

TO JIM IN SAWYER, MINNESOTA

Check out the dead cedars in the enclosed photo.
Brother—that's where I saw it.
Last week. A light snow had started to fall
and then changed into a blizzard.
The soft, fat snowflakes came
at my Thunderbird's windshield
like a million shooting stars
and gave me fearful vertigo.
I slowed down to a crawl
and then something big
danced in my headlights.
I thought it might be a cow, but it wasn't.
It was man-shaped and huge.
Over six feet tall. Covered with hair.
Could've been one of your relatives . . .
Completely covered with dark hair
and wearing high heels.
Yeah, by those dead cedars is where I saw it.
Last week. A light snow had started to fall
and soon changed into a blizzard.
Brother, that night I was seven years sober
and looking like hell to break out.

TO BILL IN MINNEOTA, MINNESOTA

Don't say I don't know, I said to her.
Howcome you say that, I said.
I don't know, she said.
No, really, howcome you're saying
I don't know to all my questions?
I don't know, she said.
Exasperated, I asked, what *do* you know?
I don't know, she said.
Yeah, today we tussled hard and long
over her confusion, and I fell
asleep on the couch and woke up
with this Holy Man kneeling next to me.
I guess he was a Holy Man,
an ancient Eastern Holy Man . . .
maybe one of the Dalai Lama's lieutenants
or that saffron-robed Buddhist monk
who barbecued himself in 1963
or maybe he was a misplaced "ancient one"
from some New Age mutant network,
but he was alive—Alive, I say.
Are you okay, he asked?
I don't know, I said. You tell me.
He stood behind me in a gentle, cosmic
warmth and asked if I believed in God.
No, I said. Are you kidding or what?
He smiled and gently caressed
my lower left ribcage, separated the flesh
and inserted his hand against my heart.
The S.O.B. squeezed all love out of my heart.

NOTE TO A YOUNG REZ ARTIST

Hey, I thought they were eagles circling
above, a good luck sign for Skins, but closer
inspection revealed them to be the turkey
vultures of broken English.

Hey, I remember once you sent me
a hand-scrawled note saying you were out
of typewriter ribbons and I sent you off
fifty bucks that same day
and you wrote back saying you got
the ribbons and some Big Macs to boot.

Young brother, now I'm puzzled
down to the core of my sour-wine soul.
I'm mired in middle age
and you're becoming famous
before your time and I'd envy you
except that I, too, thought
I knew what red pain was
in my mad-groined, goofball twenties.
Thought I knew how to bareback
this mother called Earth.

COYOTE'S CIRCLE

for Linda, who ended up East

I

In South Dakota and heading
west, Coyote was hurtling down
the highway and wishing
for a drink, watching a fly trapped
inside the air-conditioned tomb
smash its head again and again
against the invisible God
of the windshield, so he stopped
his Thunderbird and chased
the fly from front to back
with his cigarette lighter
until the concept wearied him
and he wasted it with his fist.

II

Near Provo, Utah, the squeaky
clean, hardass State Storm Trooper
who pulls Coyote over for speeding
also fines him for not wearing his seat
belt and glares at his brilliant white
dentures on the front seat.
He tells Coyote to remove
the eagle feather dangling
from his rearview mirror
because it "impedes vision"
and to put his choppers back
into his hairy head.
"What kinda feather?" the cop asks,
and Coyote says, "Turkey."
Coyote bites his lip to keep from
giggling or starting a shootout
in the loopy land of Brigham Young.
Oy vey, these people claim Indians to
be one of the lost tribes of Israel.
Coyote's fangs pierce his lip

and he smiles at the taste
of his own warm, canine blood.
Nothing matters, he's headed for home.
Home, where his ancestors lie buried.

III

Home, northern Nevada. July baking.
He's zipping down the desert interstate
between Lovelock and Fernley
when a spew of foam in the corner
of his eye shoots ten feet into the air
and Coyote's got the only car around
so he slams on the brakes.
He shakes his head to make sure
he's not having an acid flashback
and prays that the oddity of a geyser
on the barren, baked land won't be
a precursor to alien spaceship landings.
He slowly backs the car up the hot tar
until he comes to the spot where white
foam shot high into the sky.
He gets out with pistol in hand
and sees three cans of Coors
on the scorched sand.
One has exploded
and the other two
are due any second.
Coyote releases the safety
and fires, freeing warm spirits
born to be ice-cold.

Beer, blood, soil, home.

So many lost years connecting crazy.
So many lost years connecting crazy
and love and memories
and love and forgotten memories.

DEAD REZ LAND DREAM

I

The Rez land we wanted was thick
with cottonwood and occasional
bands of white pine. It had
natural springs that bubbled down
creeks to a green pond filled with catfish.
We said the land we wanted would swarm
with paint ponies, pigeons, and chickens.
We would build a large log house on a hill
exploding with wild cherry and sunflowers.
Our log house would throb with Dylan
tapes and warmth from a fireplace.
Our log house would be stuffed to
the rafters with cats and dogs from
the Animal Rescue in Rapid City.
There would be a large library filled
with all your books on education,
art, and teaching, and all the books
I wrote in which I set up situations,
pointed my finger, and laid blame . . .
But this is a dead Rez land dream.
I can hear our souls rustling
like the dry corn of autumn.
I can taste my heart as it crawls
to my throat when the strange girl
I live with forgets what I remember
was all we ever wanted.
Land, a log home, love, and peace.
The horseshit of a halfbreed existence.

II

Now returns that dream of childhood.
I'm atop a rocky hill in the desert.
Dismounted cavalry are flanking me,
firing up from all sides.
I only have a bow, but then a miracle happens.

I whip out a Thompson submachine gun
with a huge wheel clip and start to
mow the bluecoats down.
Willie Boy or Charles Whitman . . .
Walt Whitman, what's the difference?

MEDICINE SONG

Because all my Alzheimer's books say
I should, I take a self-mandated respite.
I leave my woman with her nieces
and take ten days away from
my daily allegiance to dementia.
It's April Fool's Day and weak snow
is pelting the T-Bird but not sticking
to the road and I'm shooting
down the Medicine Bow
with Laramie in sight.
The clouds break and the sun spokes
down shafts of gold, and I wish
I could reach through the windshield
and grab that white dog God
by the nape of his neck
and shake him till the fleas
of human pain and dysfunction
no longer linger, no longer
are ready to be imparted
to those created
in his blank-ass image.

Two days later I'm at the Indian Cemetery
in Lovelock, Nevada. I'm up
on a black rock volcanic bluff,
near an ancient dump, and I'm talking,
crying, pulling old sticks and weeds
off my sleeping relations, sleepy myself,
when off to my right, a hundred yards
away some white dudes
with stereo blasting rap-crap
are four-wheeling over the sage
and I glare at their rapidly
disappearing dustcloud and see
that their genes will always whisper:
"Take, take, take."

Once, my woman would have understood
the sad irony of this scenario immediately.
Now I could slowly explain it ten times
or more and she would not get it.
Still, she would smile sweetly and say,
"Sure, of course I understand you."
O Grandfather, is my life to be miserable
from here on in? More miserable
than the miserable it has always been?
This self-pity is the worst part, yet
it feels natural and right.
Grandfather, give my sleeping relations peace.
Grandfather, give my woman a forgetfulness
of her forgetfulness.
There is no other medicine
I know of except one
I cannot or will not now say.

GOOD MORNING AMERICA

Last week on "Good Morning America"
I heard the host heifer Joan Lunden
say of her guest Michael Bolton that
"He puts the soul in soul music!"
Christ almighty, Big Vanilla Mikey
ain't got an ounce of soul
in his bleached blonde bloomers.
In America at this turn of the century
the only people with soul
are hiding out and waiting.
Near the previous *fin de siècle,*
in 1912, Jim Thorpe received
his soon-to-be-repossessed Olympic gold
medals from the King of Sweden.
Burt Lancaster, who plays him in the movie,
says, "Thank you, your Majesty."
But I know Jim Thorpe really (and simply
savagely) said, "Thanks, King."
It leaves a sour taste on my tongue to marry
Thorpe and Bolton in the same mouthful.
Soul brother Bolton is a singing clown.
Poor Jim Thorpe died of booze and stolen gold.
Deep down in the bowels of our televisions,
America swims in the electric drool
of self-inflicted dementia.

STAR QUILT IN A PAWNSHOP

That sure looks like the same star quilt.
It was so many years ago I can barely remember.
There were dozens of *canli wapahte,* the small
cloth tobacco ties around the room.
And the smell of sage was overpowering.
The two helpers wrapped the quilt around
the *yuwipi* man and tied him up with rope.
Then the lamps went out.
Colored lights danced and spritzed
like sparklers above our heads
and a live buffalo walked among us.
It stepped on my foot
and I couldn't walk for a week.
Darling, I can't remember if
that's the same star quilt.
Can you? Wait—wait.
Never mind. Forget it.

CEREMONIES OF THE DAMNED

Now I gather photographs of skies
and paste them down.
This paper country of clouds,
this artifice, as near as I,
unbeliever, can lean toward heaven.
—Joanne de Longchamps

Sweetheart . . .
Almost two years now since your diagnosis.
This morning I sent you to the dumpster
in the back yard with a bag of newspapers.
Empty it, bring the bag back I said, but
you returned beaming, the bag still full.
I sent you back again. Again the full bag
followed you back inside.
The third time the same, so the fourth
I took it myself cussing all the way.
Sometimes you forget my words
before they froth from my mouth.
It's been two slow years of disintegration.
Except for madness, it's been mostly uneventful.

❖

This month the days crept into weeks
like green mold on Wonderbread.
I sat in my Stratolounger, one eye watching
my wife evaporate; the other eye noting
the disease of spreading gangs on the news.
On the first day of the second week
in October I went to the Post Office
and stood in line
behind a Methodist woman.
I knew she was Methodist because she asked
for the mail for the Methodist Church.
No, don't call me Sherlock or Mr. Lonely . . .
She was tall, light-hued for a Skin,
and wore polyester slacks.
Her upper half was slight, small breasts

and thin arms, but her backside
was out of a Rubens painting.

Holy-roly-poly God, her ass was bountiful,
shimmering, sacred and beautiful—my eyes
bugged out—and I knew if I could just rest
my head on it and use it for a pillow
all my dreams would come true.
Our bills would be paid, my blood
pressure would return to normal, my missing
teeth would grow back, I might even get an
occasional lusty urge, and my wife
would regain her brain and be sane.
Such was the power of that woman's flesh.
No, such was the power of my own
reawakening flesh!
Sweet Christ, my high plains world
was bathed in the clarity
of my brand-new yellow lenses
and the soft hush of Ativan.

I thought of that woman
all the way home and she made me hungry.
I made cold chicken sandwiches when I
reached the house, but we were out of mayo.
I'd eaten mayonnaise all my life
but that bright fall morning I made
the decision to switch to Miracle Whip.
I sped to the grocery store, made my wife
stay in the car as I bought a family-size jar.
The next week I fed my wife Miracle Whip
with tuna, bologna, bacon and tomato,
egg salad, ham, Spam, and potato salad.

Sometimes it's hard to comprehend that
ceremonies of the damned are useless.
We came to like the sweet taste, but when
the jar was empty I bought plain old mayo.
Who dares to say this hellhole
we live in is truly the land of the free?

BLACK CROW DREAMS

When the last red man shall have perished from the earth
and his memory among the white man shall have become a myth,
these shores shall swarm with the invisible dead of my tribe . . . At
night when the streets of your cities and villages shall be silent, and
you think them deserted, they will throng with the returning hosts
that once filled and still love this beautiful land.
—Chief Seattle

I

Dear Chief Seattle:
I was wondering if you ever ran into
Kurt Cobain in your travels
upon the spirit road.
I mean, I've lived five hundred
and eighty-eight moons, and, wait—

This just in from Rushville, Nebraska.
Here, Skins haunt the sidewalks
every howling Friday night.
And even today, on Main Street
the week after New Year's Eve,
a flock of red-eyed pigeons
is just being released from the city jail.

Down my street, by a white picket fence
with sidewalks neatly cleaned of snow,
four Indian girls are drinking
something from a bottle and giggling.
Oh, how I want some.
Oh, how I crave them,
but a black crow cackling
is counting my years and smirking.

II

I've lived five hundred and eighty-eight moons.

Winter litters my yard
with old bones and frozen dog turds.
My cedars are frosted white

like artificial Christmas trees.
The fat, squawking crow in the lower
branches knocks bough
snow down on me.
It is the sign of the Messiah.
Not Jesus Christ, but big-hatted
Wovoka Jack Wilson from Mason Valley,
Nevada, where I lettered in football
and bucked bales to buy school clothes
three hundred and sixty moons ago.
Despite the cliché, I wince
when I think of the boy that I was.

III

Winter litters my old bones
with the ghosts of my young soul.
My cedars are tired and gangly.
They need trimming.
Out the corner of my eye,
a sinewed something leaps
from the trees near my house.
Its fangs drip blood
but my stone axe is trained.
Two flapping crows carry
my stuttering heart up
through quite godless clouds.

IV

I've lived five hundred and eighty-eight moons.

I don't know much, except
this is the Rez and ninety-nine percent
of the people in America
could never fathom how life is here.
I will tell you that one night
during my endless drinking years,
I saw the kindest girl in the world
buying peanuts at the liquor store.
Later, staggering around in the black,

moonless night, I heard
a whirring in the sky.
A flock of crows landed on me
and carried me across town.
They dropped me down
inside her bedroom.
I sat on her bed and watched her undress
and then I fell deep asleep.
I awoke fourteen years later,
my morning mouth full
of black feathers,
eternal fear,
forlorn hope, and restless love.

Are our wings broken, darling?
Or have we simply forgotten
how-the-Christ to fly?

A COLOSSAL AMERICAN COPULATION

for Scarecrow

They say there's a promise
coming down that dusty road.
They say there's a promise coming
down that dusty road, but I don't see it.
So, fuck the bluebird of happiness.
Fuck the men who keep their dogs chained.
Fuck the men who molest their daughters.
Ditto the men who wrap their dicks
in the Bible and then claim the right
to speak for female reproductive organs.
Likewise the men who hunt coyotes.
And the whining farmers who get paid
for not growing corn and wheat.
The same to the *National Enquirer.*
Also Madonna (Santa Evita, indeed).
Yes, add the gutless Tower of Babel
that they call the United Nations.

Fuck every gangbanger in America.
Fuck furiously the drive-by shooters,
the carjack thugs, the Colombian coke cartels.
And the ghost of Richard Milhous Nixon.
Okay, add the yuppie-hillbillies who mess up
the powerspray carwash when they come down
from the hills with half the earth clinging
to their new four-wheel drives.
Fuck my neighbor who beats his kids.
And my other neighbor who has plastic
life-sized deer in his front yard.
And Tommy's Used Cars in Chadron, Neb.

Fuck my high school coach for not starting
me in the '64 State Championship game.
Fuck the first bar I puked in.
That first cigarette I ever smoked.
That first pussy I ever touched.

Fuck it again, Sam.
And that know-it-all Larry King
and his stupid suspenders.
Fuck the Creative Writing programs
and all the Spam poets they hatch.
And the air that blew Marilyn Monroe's
dress up over her waist.
Fuck you very, very much.
Fuck the Bureau of Indian Affairs.
The ATF for the Waco massacre.
And sissy boy George Will.
And Sam Donaldson's wig.
Fuck the genocidal Serb soldiers;
may their nuts roast in napalm hell.
Fuck all the booze I ever drank. Yes, include
the hair of the dog that bit me for
more than twenty drunken years.

Fuck a duck!
And the '60s and all that righteous reefer.
Fuck James Dean and his red jacket.
John Wayne and the gelding
American horse he rode in on.
The IRA and their songs and bombs.
All the Gila monsters in Arizona.
Bob Dylan for leading me astray
for three misty, moping decades.
My gall bladder for exploding.
Fuck *The Wasteland* by T. S. Eliot
and all those useless allusions.
Fuck war in every form and all other clichés.
Fuck, no, double-fuck the Vietnam War.
Every cruel act I ever committed.
Every random act of kindness.
And the undertaker who will gaze
upon my dead and naked flesh
and wince at my lack of tattoos.
Fuck O. J. Simpson and his Ginsus.
Fuck Jesse Helms, and when he dies,

wormfuck him good in his grave.
Fuck the prairie dogs.
The mosquitoes.
The immaturity of MTV.
Those Monster Trucks.
Mother Teresa. Jesus, just kidding.
The Information Superhighway.
F*U*C*K the L*A*N*G*U*A*G*E poets
and fuck rodeo cowboys in their chapped
and bony butts and boots.
Fuck the gutless Guardsmen
who were at Kent State; may they still
have night horrors after all these years.

Fuck all those, who because of this and that
and a touch of cowardice on my part,
I neglected here to name.
Fuck Alzheimer's Disease.
And all the things my woman
cannot remember.
Fuck all the things my woman
cannot comprehend.
And time. It only confuses her.
Fuck dog spelled backwards.
And fucking. We don't do it anymore.
And death. Almost an afterthought.
Fuck it. Fuck it short and tall.
Fuck it big and small.
Fuck it all.
Fucking A. Fuck me.
Never mind. I'm already fucked.

They say there's a promise
coming down that dusty road.
They say there's a promise coming down
that dusty road, but I don't see it.

BLACK IS THIS NIGHT OF LOVE

"I hope we make it home
before this storm," I say.
"I hope we make it home
before this storm," you say.
Me: "It's gonna be bad."
You: "It's gonna be bad."
It's incredibly black, black beyond
metaphor just before the blizzard hits.
Late March, late night in the car
near Bordeaux Creek, in the pines
between Chadron and Rushville.
The trunk of our new used LeSabre
is pregnant with supplies,
mostly TV dinners from Safeway
since I do all the cooking now
and the Blue Oyster Cult anthem
"Don't Fear the Reaper"
is rocking the oldies station.
I reach over, pretend to muss your hair
but really I'm holding down
the dark balloon that is your head.
You wiggle your skull from my hand.
"Sometimes you really get on my nerves,"
I say and reach for your hand
thinking of the three times tonight
you wandered off in the grocery store.
"Sometimes you really get on my nerves,"
you say and squeeze my hand back.
"I love you," I say.
"I love you," you say.
"Are you just mocking me?" I ask.
I can't see your eyes, not that it would help.
"Sometimes you get on my nerves," you say.
You let go of my bloodless hand.
"What's wrong?" I ask.
"I don't know," you say.
"Really, what's wrong?"

Again you say you don't know.
"Okay," I say. "Let's do the tables.
How much is six times six?"
You: "Sixty-six."
"Five times five?"
You: "Ninety-five."
"That's wrong. What's five times five?"
"I don't know," you answer.
"Shit," I yell, exasperated.
Searing, sizzling sad, I crank up
the Blue Oyster Cult and fill the void
until the white swirling blizzard hits.
Somewhere in the blinding snow
I feel your hand on my shoulder.
"I love you," you say.
"I doubt it," I say,
a pitiful big man pouting in darkness.
"I love you," you say, and I shudder
and reach for your hand.
It is warm and you are *wakan.*

IT HAS COME TO THIS

Three days a week I imprison you
among the shrieking aged,
the palsied pukers, the damned
and abandoned, the certifiably insane.
I do this because I am weak
and I think I'm going crazy, too.
This logical step, this "adult daycare"
at the Parkview Nursing Home
fills me with guilt. It has come to this
and soon will be worse.
Darling, I would hope you'd do
the same were our roles reversed.
Just drop me
into that writhing snakepit
and let the fanged slitherers
slide down my throat, coil briefly
inside the dry blackness of my skull,
and then shoot moaning, out of my mouth
the snakiest lonesome blues on Earth.

GETTING A SECOND OPINION

I've just bought you a new winter coat
and we're temporarily sane,
cruising two blocks down the street
from K-Mart in Rapid City.
Three young Indian boys,
fourteen, maybe fifteen years
old and living the thug life
are strolling across the busy street
making cars stop and I slam on
the brakes and give them the finger
and they flash gang signs and one pulls
a small silver gun and I stomp on the gas
and in the rearview mirror I see them
laughing, and I know positively
by the fear in your eyes that
not only is the white man's God
dead, but the Great Spirit is too.

SHALL WE GATHER AT THE RIVER

Everything comes full circle.
Cruising up Main Street I nearly
hit the old yellow bus
from the nursing home
because I'm lost in the ether
of high school girls strolling.
The heads of the old folks,
somehow miniaturized
bob up and down
in the rattletrap bus.
You are the youngest,
sitting up front, bleary behind
the soft, shameless tears
of this lame poem here
and now. Last night I drove by
our old house and peeked in the windows.
We were inside, young, drunk
and in everlasting love.

FOR YOU, THESE FLOWERS

Caught in slow motion for several
years now, I thought the final phase
would be more seasonal.
But it's here now, abrupt, shimmering
in multicolored madness.
The snows have melted, and all manner of crazed
flowers burst from your mouth and ears.
Blue wildflowers clutter the carpet.
Bloodred roses clamber up the walls
and copulate in profound confusion.
Yellow sunflowers fill the fridge.
Our dogs and cats are covered with lilacs.
Forget-me-nots bloom upon the ceiling.
Crazed geraniums sprout from the
phone when you answer it.

Our world smells so funereal
that now I finally see
I no longer have the chance
to say all the little things I forgot
to say during our years together.
Darling, there are so many little pictures
I could paint for you
if raging peonies didn't fill your skull
and confuse your eyes.

I could tell you the songs
my stepfather's razor strop sang.
I could polish the memory of my first car,
a baby blue '57 Ford Fairlane.
I could try to describe the magnificent
break of my high school curveball.

Just for the hell of it, I could speak of 1968
and me, walking circles in the snow,
hungover, kicked out of the brick
Back Bay apartment where lived

the woman who looked like Baez.
Winter hell was buffeting Boston, and war
and love raged all across this nation.
Sweetheart, I could describe how silent
ice flowers formed on my moustache
and how my hair was long even then.
I wore a pea coat,
Navy surplus bellbottoms,
always carried ZigZags,
a small bottle of patchouli
and never-never-never dreamed
I would live to be this old
and be suffocated by flowers.

MARIO SAVIO

Here in America, as I stand
on the rickety bridge to the next century,
I believe that true madness shouldn't be
a subject for poems, but damn it,
I'm sitting in my car in a snowstorm, engine
running, parked in front of the house, listening
to a Leo Kotke tape with my dog Goggles.
I am simply seeking breath.
The love of my life is possessed by the devil.
She's inside, in the lifeboat of our bed with all
our silverware, freshly opened bars of soap,
dozens of pens, hundreds of old photos
and negatives, half-eaten apples, hard Christmas
candies, and, sweet Jesus, all her jewelry
piled under the sheets. When I go in,
I fully expect her to sit up in bed, swivel
her head one hundred and eighty degrees,
and vomit split-pea soup.

Goggles is napping with her head on my lap
and I'm trying to recall the taste of Tanqueray
with a hint of vermouth and a cocktail onion.
Sometimes when you really love
a dog, it will get hit by a car, its stomach
pouch peeled back, its intestines
steaming on the hot pavement,
but it will live. Sometimes when you really
love a dog, shavehead white gangster trash
down the street will poison it
with hamburger soaked in antifreeze
and it will live.
Sometimes when you really love a dog,
it can act as a radio receiver for the voice
of Jehovah, or more frightening, sometimes
it can be one of those gray, blackeyed
aliens in disguise . . .
By all that is holy, what I say now

is the uncut truth.
From the thrashing helm of my couch
earlier this day, I heard the television
announce the death of Mario Savio
and I spasmed when my dog pounced
on my chest and screeched deep
into my halfbreed brain cells.
Stick a needle in my eye and hope to die,
I swear Goggles howled Marrr—eee—ooo!
We are all possessed here.
There is no exorcist in sight.
And Mario Savio is dead.

11-5-96

THIS IS THE REZ

This is the Rez.
Many times the luminous legions
of night driving cars
will only have one headlight.
These are the notorious "one-eyed Fords."
Sometimes driving a deserted stretch
in the black crow night, a black car
with no headlights at all will roar
past you at a hundred miles an hour.

Then you know that this *is* the Rez.
Wild Indian ghost cars and more.
Wild Indian ghost cars and less.

Skin memories fading.
Skin memories being created.
Love impossible. Love still possible?